LISTFUL LIVING

LISTFUL LIVING

Transforming Your Life One List at a Time

JULES HAWTHORNE

RWG Publishing

CONTENTS

1	Introduction	1
2	The Power of Lists	3
3	Creating Effective Lists	4
4	Organizing Your Life with Lists	6
5	Listful Living for Productivity	8
6	Listful Living for Personal Growth	10
7	Listful Living for Health and Wellness	12
8	Listful Living for Relationships	14
9	Listful Living for Finances	16
10	Listful Living for Time Management	18
11	Listful Living for Goal Setting	20
12	Listful Living for Stress Management	22
13	Listful Living for Self-Care	24
14	Listful Living for Travel Planning	26
15	Listful Living for Home Organization	27
16	Conclusion	29

Copyright © 2024 by Jules Hawthorne

All rights reserved. No part of this book may be reproduced in any manner whatsoever without written permission except in the case of brief quotations embodied in critical articles and reviews.

First Printing, 2024

CHAPTER 1

Introduction

Using and creating a list, in a meaningful way, is transformative. This is not a self-help book in the usual sense. There is not one correct way of doing things. This is a deeply reflective and fact-based exploration of the most efficient tools we can use to create meaningful change in our lives. In the end, making life joyful is the goal — which happens as a result of clarity on the most meaningful tasks. Each list creates awareness and insight. It challenges us to pay attention, it invites our own alignment of our time, our spirit, our intellect, and our surroundings. This integration among the quiet and the loud, the grand and the small, the universal and the intimate, makes it congruent. With congruence comes focus. With focus comes transformation. When we use lists in the way we'll be sharing with you, things become easier, simpler, gentler, and certainly more fun.

Many people consider their lives hectic and unmanageable because they are overwhelmed with the amount of things they have to do. Time feels like an unending struggle to keep up, and joy feels like something that everyone else has managed to claim, but that remains elusive in your life. It can be hard to believe that there's enough light and goodness in the universe to shine on you. We don't think that. We know that the light is there for everyone. We only need to open our senses to it. We need to create order, openings for finding joy, peace, wonder, and forgiveness, and so much more.

CHAPTER 2

The Power of Lists

The first tool I discovered for listful living is list visualization. This is a tool that uses the universal law of the universe, intention, combined with solution-focused psychology. Your list is actually a visual representation of your desires, acting as the first step in creating change in your life. It's like a dream board, but with a to-do list. Instead of feeling overwhelmed by everything you think you "should" or "have to" do, you can instead translate that into what you want to do. What you need to do. And then you visualize how to do it. And, just like in a movie, once you see the end, the next steps seem to appear simply. It's in you.

When most people think about lists, they think of a tool for grocery shopping, errands, or tasks. Lists help people to record and organize information. They help the brain to prioritize and to translate the insurmountable into the possible. But that grossly underestimates the power of the list. My journey began with a very long list that took months to write, and I discovered something profound about this very boring task. This simple activity can change your life.

CHAPTER 3

Creating Effective Lists

Third, lists are linear in nature, meaning that you write and read them, typically, line by line from top to bottom. This may seem like a very basic point, but it's crucial to mention. I want to emphasize this notion because someone may look at a list and immediately think either that the first is the most important, or that the last item is the point of completion. These can both be true, of course. However, the vast majority of the time this is not how lists are constructed. I can't say, for instance, that your priority in writing this paragraph should be item number 1 instead of the last point. At the same time, I can't say that one is more important. Yes, there is a sequence. However, I believe that most lists, properly ordered, have been written in this way in order to most effectively communicate the qualities and associated quantities meant to be conveyed. Therefore, every item on it is equally important vis-à-vis the other items on the list. What I mean to emphasize is not that multiple yet equal emotions, desires, or objectives are addressed in a short list but rather that all of these things received a quantifiable value that must be met in order for them to be accounted for and simultaneously managed in time effectively.

With all this talk of lists, you might wonder if there is a secret that makes lists really work or live up to their touted benefits. The answer to that is not any single thing per se, but rather a combination of qualities. First, lists are concise. You can get lost in long lists, get confused, and overlook things. Now, if you're someone who loves to write things out fully and in depth in order to thoroughly think things through and find clarity through that process, you don't have to forgo that completely. You can instead make your larger list on a separate written page and then use your list to break that down into smaller, more focused lists that are easier to work through. Second, lists are objective. This means that they don't capture feelings but facts and objectives. Lists as a reflection of your values and attributes bring everyone closer to the same playing field. In other words, because they are factual, they can be used as a common language between us. This maximizes our potential, aligning all those involved to understand and act in unity while minimizing our differences.

CHAPTER 4

Organizing Your Life with Lists

Whether you are a single millennial working in the city or a baby-boomer with a history of responsibilities that make it seem as if you are carrying the weight of the world on your shoulders, staying current with modern technology and creating lists to help you fulfill the responsibilities of your life, no matter how diverse they are, can be the first steps in finding a sense of unity and balance in your life. Corporate executives, remote workers, single stay-at-home moms, and married fathers of three children all have potentially diverse, overwhelming, yet wonderfully unique lives. No category of my preceding examples has a realistic understanding of everything in life. Each has unique responsibilities, and there are infinite ways to live a rough, stressful, and chaotic life. Nevertheless, all people who are looking to create a better version of their lives have a place to start. Lists build upon the strengths of every individual and can be used to help eliminate all the clutter that an often hectic and disorganized life can create.

Listful living doesn't happen in a vacuum. It depends on each of us being organized enough to make our lists work for us. Life is busy. Sometimes life is great, and sometimes life is challenging. There are times when life can be so frantic that trying to keep track of all of the important things in life, while also trying to ensure that we continue to positively evolve as humans, can be extraordinarily intense.

CHAPTER 5

Listful Living for Productivity

With the growth of hyperconnectivity and a common belief in the wisdom of abundant resources, we're bombarded with external influences. We're also likely to feel the need to say yes to too many things, instead of saying no to most things in order to maintain our sanity. Chad Grills argues that in a world where hyperconnectivity and instant access generate discontentment and media-induced envy, focus is the new IQ. In reality, the foundational principle of achieving success and happiness in our lives is not the concept of specific goals or new and novel thinking as the solution: it is changing the way we think about our nuanced relationship with the perpetual, undifferentiated, and ultimately limited resource of time. This isn't just about productivity. It's about quality of life, and arguably even the systemic changes we might be able to make within society at large, reinforced by individual attitude adjustment. A managed, more disruptive approach to "what goes," may encourage a mindset that reaffirms and aligns our actions with the ultimate value of what we do, see, experience, and feel.

When the term FOMO, or fear of missing out, was officially added to the Oxford dictionary in 2009, daily affirmations went into overdrive. Whether you're phone-free, fasting from technology, or off the grid (I feel like I should ask if the world is still there when people take their tech health vacations), the same anxiety-provoking narrative runs through all these conversations: I'm going to miss something essential. When the experience you are afraid of missing out on is life itself, the stakes feel pretty high. Today's hyperconnectivity is psychologically addictive.

CHAPTER 6

Listful Living for Personal Growth

In addition, as I mentioned above, if you list, you should also "not list". Instead of filling your pie with mini rests that only take a few seconds - a short burst of activity, resting one's head or playing mini "reward" games - it should now include some real time for rest and relaxation. Even the "most cutting-edge" fitness experts agree that the evidence for "taking regular breaks may have links to improved mental well-being". For some people, even those who are very minimal, this means that you can spend 3% of your 100% of your time on "no matter what". Do not think about your others when you are present enough - a few minutes spent on the patio or listening to music will provide the necessary space to think with a break from the busyness just as needed.

Finally, no Listful Living guide would be complete without discussing how list making can be used to become a better you. Most of us use lists to be more organized, efficient, and productive in other areas of our life. However, this is one of the areas where we typically - oh, the irony - do not utilize lists. Therefore, take time to create lists that help you with personal goals in self-improvement, self-care, mindfulness, relaxation, play, and adventure. You should include such aspects of life as spending time with the people whom you care most about, finding peace in both your home and your heart, and making time for pastimes that make you happy and whole.

CHAPTER 7

Listful Living for Health and Wellness

We all have occasional spurts of productivity - we have deadlines to meet, or big social events, or a house that needs to be cleaned for a new housemate. Some may even thrive on this pressure. But eventually, the housemate will clean the house. Even elated events have their reality check: I've mentioned the wretched feeling I regularly confront as I watch the post-vacation photos flood in around me. No one can maintain 35 days of housework in 60 hours. Real sustainable progress comes from making many small consistent changes. To do this, you need to see beyond your present reality - see where everything is headed to help make plenty of those small changes as the future unfolds. Before you can do that, you must become aware of your patterns: when you consistently make poor choices, and in those moments when your self-care has slipped, and ask yourself what the impact of these choices is - if they're leading you for your greater good, or if they're burying you in initial euphoria and long-term tedium. Here's a useful tool for visualizing that greater reality: when you're struggling to make a good choice, use your health and well-being as your priority point of reference, and list reasons why you want to make a change. Write a handful of bullet points, each pointing toward one aspect of your health, with causal, situational, and impact responses. This forces you to see beyond your current worldview and towards the greater reality of a better life. And once you've gathered these nuggets, you can make these reasons visible to yourself visually, referring to them each time you're struggling to make a difficult health-centric decision that requires the careful selection of emotional fuel.

Depressingly, the majority of us spend more time planning a vacation than we do looking after ourselves. I know I'm guilty of this. Sitting at my desk, banging on about being productive, is a prime example of not walking the talk. Bad habits slip in over time, so we're often unaware of the true extent of the problem until the repercussions start to show. Even the way we use lists can hold insights into our bad habits. Meanwhile, our physical health is in pieces, as studies indicate the importance of recognizing when we're sick. Too many of us favor the 'work hard, play hard' lifestyle, even if we're ultimately choosing to party hard in celebration of someone else's hard work. Many of us neglect our physical health because we fall into a glorification of 'busyness', follow the example of, and even derive our self-worth by being, 'busy' people. In his book "In Praise of Slowness," Carl Honoré notes that 'busy' has become a buzzword and a badge of honor to many of us in the digital age. Peppering social media updates with protests around how busy we are is no longer enough; we need our busyness validated with 'likes' and encouraging comments. We are told that the reason we aren't good enough is because we don't micro-manage our time well enough. But the more we live by our technology, the less time we have for everything in our non-virtual reality, including taking the time to look after ourselves.

CHAPTER 8

Listful Living for Relationships

Living with someone when you're super organized can be tough, especially if your partner is the opposite. When is my turn to cook? How can he stop asking me where the black shirt is? Now he knows if he doesn't see it on the list, he can ask. And I'm working on making the list readily available, even if it's not always on my phone. Anyone that comes into this apartment should know from the get-go that there's a hub for any food, social activity, chore, and/or pertinent communication. Keep working on it so that it becomes more habitual and pleasant for everyone involved.

I used to make my grocery list a couple of hours beforehand, and then the act of feeling prepared helped me feel more settled. Now Greg and I sit down for 20 minutes every Saturday morning and plan out all of our meals and who will do the cooking and the grocery shopping. Sometimes we alternate picking out the recipes, and sometimes we do a cooking "marathon" where we plan out 4 or 5 recipes during the week that use the same basic ingredients - like chicken! On busier weekends, we'll make weekend breakfast the meal of choice and make something more fun or extravagant than the usual pancake or yogurt bowl.

CHAPTER 9

Listful Living for Finances

5. Interest rate card: Before closing an interest rate card, making interest claims, and transferring credit benefit balances to a new card, you can make a list of 2-50 toll-free numbers of the lenders needing to be transferred to successfully have a win-win for yourself and the right lenders.

4. Credit pre-list: Sometimes when things start to lull in the economy, it is not unusual for lenders to alter the terms of credit benefits. A pre-list of favorable account changes can protect you when credit lenders hike.

3. Personal credit report: A list of the credit-reducing actions you can list and investigate.

2. Money management: A list of collection of things you do in order to start making your money work for you.

1. Plan to invigorate your credit: List things that will help you to speedily advance the most important aspects of your beneficial credit card/credit scores.

Here are a few ideas for lists to get you started on managing your personal finances:

Using your handy dandy list-making methods, you can create the only thing richer than your checking account – a personal financial plan! List definitions of main and short-term personal financial safety and success. Define how you intend to acquire money, save it, and spend it. Develop a personal budget, saving, and expense plans. You can then list long, medium, and short-range money objectives. Calculate how these objectives are met within your own time limit and interpret the results when comparing with actual revenues received and costs incurred. List your tolerable personal hazards and work up risk management plans. Each financial goal or plan will have its own list, which should be visited and combined with others periodically.

Build a "Personal Financial Plan"

CHAPTER 10

Listful Living for Time Management

You can create a "molecular" to-do list composed of all your small tasks, and you can accomplish them one by one. It's a fact of life that we want more and more out of our days. Having a good list gives a semblance of control over the future. To have control might be frustrating in the eye of a control freak, but it's also rewarding. This is one of the dirtiest and deepest little secrets when it comes to getting things done. Most who have to answer to a superior are forced to reconcile with this truth. The process of writing a list is a mental clarification of reality. You visualize things in words, affixed, in a certain order, to a piece of paper. When it's written down, you can process things. It makes it seem all the more manageable, even when it isn't. In some ways, it makes things easier.

If you want to increase your personal productivity, start making more lists. No amount of advanced technology can replace the simple beauty of a well-crafted list. Whether you scrawl it on a Post-it note or swipe your iPhone, anyone can put pen to paper to improve their time management skills. Lists help prioritize. Lists transform the bigger problems and inconveniences in your life into small inconveniences. Instead of, "I don't have any food in my fridge," you can look at your shopping list and think, "Well, this will be inconvenient now, but as soon as I get to the store, I'll have everything I want."

CHAPTER 11

Listful Living for Goal Setting

Paula takes a surprising stand when it comes to sharing your dreams with others. "Not every goal should be made public. Maybe sharing your smaller, day-to-day list items keeps you focused. (It works that way for me.) But some goals—particularly those larger dreams—get a weird zing when you tell people about them. Can that excitement translate into making great strides forward toward your dreams?"

Rizzo brings a journalist's mind to the hows and whys of productivity. When it comes to big goals, she explains, "It's all about focus. You have limited resources to accomplish anything. Time, energy, money—it's all stretched. Think about what's urgent versus what's important and adjust your priorities accordingly. Be realistic about the amount of time you need to accomplish it—and then add a buffer for things that might go wrong. Reasonable expectations are the key to a less-stressed life."

Vacations, career changes, a new car, a marathon. Who hasn't daydreamed about making something big happen in the next year or so? But how many times have you tried—and failed—to set those exciting goals, only to have them fall by the wayside as soon as things get really real? As this new year gets going and resolutions are still fresh (or already fading), let's look at some new strategies for setting the cleverest, most awesome, totally successful 2019 goals.

CHAPTER 12

Listful Living for Stress Management

Clearing Brain Clutter: Having too many thoughts can seriously weigh you down, and can cause stress that neither mental nor physical power can alleviate. To prevent this, you need a quick fix to help ease your potentially stressful mental load. Fear not, fellow cluttered brains. That's exactly where listing comes in. Getting out of your spinning top of a brain, onto paper or the computer, can instantaneously neutralize many of your stressful thoughts. So, think of your lists as clutter guns instead. With every item you jot down, your stress will subsequently lessen. Circling tasks/thoughts over and over again takes too much mind strength - nobody's got time for that. In fact, my colleague, Dr. Wong, uses lists whenever she's stressed. Reviewing not only lessens her tornado brain, but creates structure in chaos. With something tangible to work from, she says, "it's a relief." For this reason, people suffering from anxiety agree that list-making can assist in stress reduction. It's not meditative; rather, repetitive, meticulous motion in listing can distract, harmonize and alleviate excessive worries.

Stress. Invariably, it's an inevitable part of life today, thanks to many of the trappings of modern living. And while stress may be a fact of life, it doesn't have to be your way of life. By keeping organized, you can also keep stress from taking over how you live, feel and (negatively) react. Don't think it's possible? It is. I'll prove it to you, one list at a time.

CHAPTER 13

Listful Living for Self-Care

1. We can feel high regard for both big achievements and smaller ones, satisfied to make listful enlightened, and taking them out, tick off our accomplishments, and hugging ourselves every time we complete a task that parting or nourish, encourages an easier way for filled comfort and self-gourmet power to leave it, listed and sometimes support us. B) Listfully, we can practice gratitude towards ourselves and the world, listing what we are feeling privileged for. C) We can use listful living to keep our priorities. This may contain "saying no" and giving up committing to extra events, meetings, and situations that turn unhealthy pressure in our already-busy lives. D) To do our part in the external world, we might list virtues, objectives, or principles we care about and the more honoring, unique opportunities to form the 'rightness' we would like to have. E) We can also use listful living to 'let think', making the time to lick wounds, exhale, and recharge. Additionally, it may imply that we set goals or methods of performance which enable us

to respect our current abilities and standpoints. F) We could create gratitude lists to honor every one of our days for qualities and events within our life, which we sometimes take for granted. Gratitude listing can be an important appreciation tool when we are feeling lowly or when we need a hurry of calm. G) We can increase our confidence and happiness indirectly by braking our lists' large tasks into microscopic, convenience ones and showing ourselves us.

What will we gain when we use listful living for self-care (or self-love)? Self-care is any activity that we do deliberately in order to take care of our mental, emotional, and physical health. Life seems to move along at a very fast pace and we do not tend to stop and take time for self-care. So, listful living for self-care is a must. From meals to facial massages, we should take care and ease down our nails to celebrate ourselves. We might also feel more highly regarded for our time unaccompanied overall, which can help boost self-esteem and self-love.

CHAPTER 14

Listful Living for Travel Planning

Listful living is all about streamlining your life, increasing efficiency, and promoting constructive, thoughtful living day in, day out. When it comes to leisure time like vacation planning, it is especially important to lighten your load as best you can. My philosophy has always been to book the tickets and make lodging reservations, and then keep the rest loosey goosey. The most fun, adventurous, and unexpectedly special trip experiences have always been grounded in the basic framework of wandering and wondering, allowing time to discover endless hidden gems. Recently, however, I realized I could take a little extra time to plan up front and lighten the "I have no particularly good agenda in Sardinia, so I guess I have to sample more gelato then", which may have led to a bit too much gelato consumption.

CHAPTER 15

Listful Living for Home Organization

Let technology work in your favor. A key step to creating habits is recognizing that it will be the reminders in your day that support your new behavior. Just as you would ask a coworker or family member to help support your new goals, let technology be the reminder in your pocket. Set a series of reminders for the first 2-5 weeks when you are trying to adjust to a new habit. Once you have established a strong habit, reduce the number of reminders from a daily to a weekly consistency. Set it and forget it and let technology remind you why you chose the habit in the first place.

The most organized people are committed to maintaining good habits. Doing so ensures they are not spending unnecessary energy on tasks that deplete resources. Build solid habits by starting slow. Pick a bedtime to walk away from electronic devices or begin meditating 5 minutes a day. As you become more successful, slowly start to add on. At four months, add one or two additional habits. At nine months, add one or two more. Stay committed to the plan.

I have a one in-one out rule for all things that come into my home. Of course, there are exceptions (sentimental things), but quite simply, if something doesn't replace something that's used regularly, it can't come in. Added bonus - your home and storage stay more organized, and parting with a non-essential item is emotional, but rewarding. You won't clutter your life with things that don't matter.

CHAPTER 16

Conclusion

The hope of Listful Living is to motivate you, to instill in you a fire to really make this incredible life of yours just the incredibly amazing life you deserve. My goal is for us to create a world where happiness is a motivation and euphoria is a goal. The paradox in teaching you this new (really rather old) way of life is in the fact that simply by living more, you are preparing yourself to end your life better. When you feel great, you can be great, and being great is, at its core, ending your life well. It might be overly simple, but that is what I believe with all of my listful heart.

In so many ways, Listful Living is about getting over yourself. It is about ridding yourself of the belief that you are too busy, too tired, or simply too important to do the things you need to do to protect your physical and mental health. It is about finding a way to work for others. To spend your days laughing more, and pouting less. To spend your free hours being kind, quirky, unapologetically brave. To spend your evenings enjoying what is outside, moving, watching, dancing, lifting, cooking, learning – simply living.

Milton Keynes UK
Ingram Content Group UK Ltd.
UKHW040740301124
451843UK00010B/227